Damone Paul Johnson

A Life Worth Rebuilding

HP
HUPOMONE PRESS
FORT WORTH, TEXAS

ISBN: 978-1-4675-3274-7
Printed in the United States of America.

Library of Congress Cataloging-in-Publication Data
Nehemiah/Damone Paul Johnson, author, 1974-
ISBN: 978-1-4675-3274-7

DEDICATION

With this my first book, I want to express my deep love and appreciation to those who have enriched my life and helped make me who I am today.

In honor of my Lord and Savior Jesus Christ, whose Word is the solid rock on which I continue to build my life.

To my grandfather, Bennie Gross, whose charm, charisma, excellent work ethic, and powerful walk with God has been an awesome blueprint of a godly man.

To my grandmother, Rosie Bell Gross; my mother, Delores J. Gross-Johnson; and my wife, Angela D. Johnson, for you are all once, twice, three times my ladies.

And to the Metropolitan New Testament Baptist Church family, who listened to these sermons on Sunday morning and whose love, support, and faithfulness continue to encourage and inspire me.

I thank God for the blessing of you all.

CONTENTS

FOREWORD

Do you sense that the work of God in your life is broken and needs repair? Do you sometimes feel deeply that the kingdom of God in your neighborhood needs to be rebuilt? Would you like to see things stand up again that have fallen down around you? This is the book for you.

Rev. Dr. Damone Johnson offers you an amazing present-tense proclamation from Nehemiah. Sometimes considered a more remote book from the period of Israel's restoration after exile, Nehemiah becomes a text message to you in these vital contemporary messages.

He was a Jew; you are probably a Gentile. He lived in 444 B.C. You live in the twenty-first century. His concern was ancient Persia and the ruined Jerusalem. Your concern rests where you live. Yet this Jewish layman reaches out across the centuries and touches your life in these provocative and intriguing messages. You will understand why rebuilding a wall in fifth-century B.C. Jerusalem speaks directly to the rebuilding of your life today. Indeed, the pages of this book will give you the assurance that you have a life worth rebuilding.

The flesh-and-blood human Nehemiah looks out at you from these pages. You feel his hurt when he hears that God's work rests in ruins. You sense the salt of his tears when he thinks of God's work reduced to a pile of rubble that was once a mighty testimony. You will be astonished how God can give resources to those who have a vision. You will marvel at his exhilarating campaign to rebuild the work of God. You will mark the reality of opposition even while you are doing the best work. Sometimes you have to stand with a sword in one hand and a trowel in the other.

At the same time, you will discover how a person with a vision is never at the mercy of a person with a mere argument. In forty-nine days Nehemiah triumphs, and the witness of God is restored. Every person has a place in the work. The rebuilding of the work of God is like planting shade trees that someone else will sit under. You will want to join the choir in Jerusalem as they stand on the rebuilt wall and sing praises to God.

With rare narrative skill and the warmth of an experienced pastor's heart, Dr. Johnson weaves together the particulars of a time long ago with the needs of life today. The resulting fabric of narrative leaves you with the assurance that you have a life worth rebuilding. Dr.

Johnson produces an account so vivid that you can feel the energy of the leader Nehemiah, smell the freshness of an early morning as eager builders gather at dawn to work, hear the hammer and chisel rap against stone, and finally see the triumph of a rebuilt work for God. You look at Nehemiah, and he looks back at you, promising that you too have a life worth rebuilding.

The preacher will find inspiration to take his own tour around the wall Nehemiah built. The layperson will get a grip on rebuilding life. We all will put this volume down with thanks for a vivid and lasting work.

Joel C. Gregory
Professor of Preaching
George W. Truett Theological Seminary
Baylor University
Waco, Texas

INTRODUCTION

On August 28, 2011, when I was serving as pastor of the Metropolitan New Testament Mission Baptist Church of Albany, New York, Hurricane Irene swept over the East Coast. The storm was so severe in the Capital District of the city, I cancelled church that Sunday. Due to the force of the high winds and heavy rain, the wall of our church kitchen caved in. Thank God no one was in the kitchen at the time. I received a call that Monday morning to come down to the church. It was unbelievable to see the wall of the kitchen exposed to the elements. We were thankful some members were able to repair the wall quick enough to keep it from further exposure. Yet the wall was still exposed and unprotected from critters, thieves, and robbers.

Walls are important. There's the Great Wall of China, which is a series of fortifications made of stone, brick, tamped earth, wood, and other material generally built along the east-to-west line across the historical northern borders of China, in part to protect the Chinese empire or its prototypical states against intrusion by various nomadic groups or military incursions by various warlike peoples or forces. There's the Great Berlin Wall. In a speech made on January 12, 1987, at the Brandenburg Gate commemorating the seven hundred and fiftieth anniversary of Berlin, President Ronald Reagan challenged Mikhail Gorbachev, then the General Secretary of the Communist Party of the Soviet Union, to tear down the wall as a symbol of increasing freedom in the Eastern Bloc. While President Reagan was able to end the Cold War without a shot being fired, he is also known for helping to tear a wall down.

Historically, walls have always been a source and witness of protection from intrusion. Whether it's a wall in the church kitchen, a wall in China, or a wall that represents military fascism and danger, a wall represents protection and strength.

Within our own lives today in America, walls are down. Even though they're not actual physical walls, certainly the walls protecting our families are down. According to the National Opinion Research Center of the University of Chicago, Christians have a divorce rate of about 42%; for religiously unaffiliated Americans, it's 50%. Among adults who have been married, one-third (33%) have experienced at least one divorce. George Bonner, owner of the Bonner Group, states that Americans have grown comfortable with divorce as a natural part of life. He further states that many young people are embracing the idea of serial marriage, in which they get married two or three times, seeking a different partner for each phase of their adult lives.

Walls are not only down in our families, but they are also down politically due to an ongoing impasse between the Congress and the President. According to *The Huffington Post*, the 112th Congress that convened January 3, 2011, through January 30, 2013, is set to go down in history as the most unproductive Congress since the 1940s.

Just as the walls are down in our families and political system, the walls are also down in our educational system. According to www.usgovernmentspending.com, in 2012 the United States spent $103.3 billion on education, while it spent $849.6 billion on defense and $8.3 billion on prisons. Education counted for only 3% of the total budget in 2012.

Moreover, our society's moral walls are down. According to *The Huffington Post*, the United States accounts for 5% of the world's population but locks up nearly 25% of the world's prisoners. And during the last two decades, state spending on prisons grew by 127%—six times the rate of spending on higher education.

Walls are down economically in our nation as well. The unemployment rate is still too high and the literacy rate still too low.

Indeed, the walls are currently down in the United States—morally, politically, and economically. Yet the good news is that broken walls can be rebuilt.

In ancient Israel, Nehemiah was known for building a wall that he felt was worth rebuilding. In 444 B.C., both the wall and the temple in Jerusalem were destroyed by the Babylonians who had invaded the nation. The temple was rebuilt by Zerubbabel, but the wall was still down. During that time the wall represented the provision, protection, and power of God. It was a witness to the greatness of God and His hand upon the life of the people. The destroyed wall meant that they were living under reproach as the laughingstock of the surrounding nations.

And so, while he was eight hundred miles away, Nehemiah inquired about the condition of his people. His brother Hanani told him that the people were under reproach because the wall was down. After receiving this negative report, Nehemiah internalized the pain. He then interceded for them before God and the king. After making the eight hundred-mile journey to Jerusalem, he investigated to find out what was going on. With insight and direction from the Lord, he inspired the leaders and involved them in rebuilding the walls and repairing the gates.

Like Nehemiah, we should inquire diligently, even though just a casual inquiry would show us that our walls are down. We should not take this situation lightly but rather internalize it and intercede for God to act on our behalf. God's Word says, "If my people, which are called by my name, shall humble themselves and pray, and seek my face, and turn from their wicked way; then will I hear from heaven, and will forgive their sin and will heal their land" (2 Chronicles 7:14 KJV).

As you investigate your life, you should be inspired to get involved in rebuilding the walls of witness, because these walls that are down really indicate that the witness of the Lord is also down in the nation. I invite you to take a journey with me to look at Nehemiah and see how he rebuilt the wall in Jerusalem so you can begin rebuilding the broken areas in your own life. Your life truly is worth rebuilding! §

Chapter 1

The Power of a Praying Leader

(Nehemiah 1:1-11)

In 1991 the United States was at war in Kuwait against Saddam Hussein. Millions of soldiers were placed strategically in various areas on the ground so that they would have strongholds. Before the foot soldiers were deployed into the enemy camp for hand-to-hand combat, however, Air Force planes were sent over first to drop bombs and missiles on various strongholds because the air attack gave a critical advantage to the ground attack.

A valuable lesson from this tactic can be applied to spiritual warfare. We're on the ground in this world, but if we pray, it will give us a better advantage. Instead of deploying the Air Force, we send up the prayer force, and it gives us a greater advantage on the earth. Prayer reaches at least three worlds at the same time. Prayer goes up to God in worship, out to man and work, and down to hell in warfare. One person has said that you can learn a lot about a person by listening to how they pray.

Nehemiah prayed nine times in thirteen chapters. Usually they were very short prayers, but he prayed out of concern for others. He wasn't a prophet or a priest.

Instead, he was a cupbearer. In other words, he was a layperson. About a hundred years after the Babylonian exile comes to an end, Nehemiah wrote his memoirs about the process of rebuilding the wall in Jerusalem.

At the time of the crisis in Jerusalem, Nehemiah was living in Sushan, the winter home of the Persian king, Artaxerxes. This place was comparable to Camp David, a retreat for the President of the United States. His brothers and friends from home visited him and shared about the great distress and miserable calamity that his people were experiencing. They were receiving ridicule and reproach because the city's walls were down and its gates burned. Nehemiah expected to hear good news, but instead he heard about shame and distress.

The walls were representative of the protection, presence, and provision of God. And now a hundred years later, the temple had been rebuilt, but the walls were still down. The enemies and the land were exposed, which was a sign that God's protection and provision weren't present. So Nehemiah internalized the pain by weeping and mourning for his people. He was praying not for himself, but out of his concern for others. In fact, his concern shaped and colored the tone and tenor of his prayer.

In verses 4 through 7, Nehemiah prayed about Judah's plight. God had warned the Hebrews in Leviticus

26 that if they obeyed Him they would prosper, but if they sinned He would destroy the land and cause them to go into captivity. (Indeed, God does discipline those whom He loves.) In his prayer Nehemiah rehearsed the sin of his people: they had not kept God's commandments, judgments, and statutes.

We're also living in a time when people refuse to obey the commands and statutes of God. Every day we hear about drive-by shootings, gang violence, murders and killings, rapes, aggravated assaults, and wars and rumors of wars. Yet we realize that just as God brought judgment upon ancient Israel, He will also bring judgment upon those who are corrupt today.

Verse 8 reveals that God had brought reproach and judgment upon those who had transgressed against Him. Israel's disobedience teaches us that sin leads to suffering. All suffering is not the result of sin, but sin will indeed lead to suffering—even secret sins. The secret sins on earth are open scandals in heaven. In fact, Romans 6:23 says that the wages of sin is death.

Dr. Harry S. Wright, pastor emeritus of the Cornerstone Baptist Church of Brooklyn, New York, tells a story about visiting a farm in his childhood with his uncle, who was getting ready to kill a hog. When he opened up the gate, the hog took off running as if he knew what was happening. His uncle aimed the rifle and shot. Li'l Harry looked up at his uncle and said, "You didn't get him. You have to keep shooting." His uncle said, "I got him." Li'l Harry said, "No, he's still running." His uncle said, "I got him, Harry." Pretty soon the pig stopped, slumped over, and died. From the moment that bullet hit the pig, life for him as he once knew it was over. He was still running, dipping and diving, slipping and sliding, but his life was over. In the same way, Satan and sin have hit some of you in the head. You may get by, but you won't get away.

Nehemiah prayed about God's promise. His prayer was not an exercise in futility, for he believed God would do this based on His promise. In verse 9 he began reiterating the promise that God made to Moses: "You said that if we sin against You, You would scatter us, and You did that. You scattered us to be slaves in Babylon. But You also said that if we repent, You would restore us. If we return unto You and keep Your commandments and do them, You will not cast us out. You will bring us back to You."

It's important that we rehearse the promises of God in prayer. We should pray back to God His promises, not that He has amnesia and can't remember, but because it jump-starts our faith. Praying this way reminds us that what God has promised and done in the past, He can still do. God can still heal us, deliver us, and set us free.

There are times when we need to download on the computers of our mind those times in the past God kept His promise by bringing us out and delivering us—just so that it will jump-start our faith now. We need to rehearse the promises and performance of God to remind us that just as God promised and performed in the past, He is also able to do it in the present.

In verse 11 Nehemiah prayed over his purpose—that the Lord would cause the king to grant his request to return to Jerusalem. Nehemiah was praying to God because he understood that the heart of the king is always in the hand of the Lord (Proverbs 21:1). Just as Pharaoh's heart was turned by God in Exodus 7 and 13, God was also able to turn the heart of King Artaxerxes.

Nehemiah trusted God with the pressing concerns on his heart. In the same way, we need to remember the words of the old hymn that says,

> What a friend we have in Jesus,
> All our sins and griefs to bear!
> What a privilege to carry
> Everything to God in prayer!
> O what peace we often forfeit,
> O what needless pain we bear,
> All because we do not carry
> Everything to God in prayer. §

Chapter 2

The Ministry of the Cupbearer

(Nehemiah 1:11—2:1)

If we are faithful over a few things, God will make us rulers over much (Matthew 25:23). God has a way of moving us from obscurity to celebrity, shifting us from the background to the forefront. It happened in the life of David, who was tending his father-in-law's sheep and field, yet was anointed to become the king of Israel. It happened in the life of Dr. Martin Luther King, Jr., who was pastoring a church in Montgomery, Alabama, but was given leadership for a bus boycott, which catapulted him to international prominence. It happened in the life of President Barack Obama, who was a community worker and constitutional lawyer, but his service propelled him to become the first U.S. President of color.

This principle is also illustrated in the life of Nehemiah, who led the people of Judah in the rebuilding of the wall. But before he was a wall builder, he was a cupbearer to the king. This was not a flashy or glamorous position, but it was vital, even though it was very dangerous. Yet it was a significant training ground to develop his character, work ethic, and trustworthiness that were all needed to lead the Jews in rebuilding the wall and repairing the gates.

In the same way, before we are promoted to various positions of prominence, we must be faithful and serve with a spirit of excellence where we are. We should bloom where we're planted. We should have the spirit and character of a cupbearer.

Notice the history of the cupbearer. The position of the cupbearer was indeed an important one. Genesis 40:11 lists his job description, which was basically overseeing the grapes that were squeezed, along with the juice poured and made into wine. After drinking and tasting the wine, the cupbearer would then place the wine in the hands of the king.

The cupbearer in Genesis 41 was the one who brought to the king's attention Joseph's dream-interpreting ability. This shows that the cupbearer not only was in a position of prominence, but also of influence. It was his influence with the king that allowed him to make the recommendation for Joseph to come before him and interpret his dream. The cupbearer had to be important and unimportant at the same time. The cupbearer was important but also impressive.

In 1 Kings 10:5, the Queen of Sheba came and saw Solomon's entourage, of which the cupbearer was very much a part. Verse 5 says that it literally took her breath away. She complimented the cupbearer by saying that the half had not been told. Yet she was impressed with the king, not the cupbearer. (To be an effective cupbearer, you had to be impressed by the king and unimpressed with yourself.)

The hallmark of the cupbearer was that he was a servant. He was in charge of the vineyard and supervised the workers, along with carefully managing the production of the wine. Yet his position was always one of service.

Nehemiah was a servant's servant. Whenever Nehemiah was ever referred to, it was always in terms of service—not by title or status, but the testimony of service. He was a servant who was sacrificial because his position inherently meant that he had to make a total commitment to the king. The only way an enemy could get rid of the king was to poison him, often through his wine or food. So the job of the cupbearer involved tasting the wine and food before giving it to the king to consume. If anyone was trying to poison the king, it would have to pass through the cupbearer first. Needless to say, the cupbearer had a very important role, but it was also a sacrificial one. Like the Secret Service agents who would take the brunt of a bullet for the President in an assassination attempt, the cupbearer would swallow the poison in the wine before it ever reached the king. This meant that he had to give his very best.

In his autobiography entitled *Why Not the Best?* former President Jimmy Carter talks about his hitch in the Navy. Once a sergeant said to him, "Carter, have you always given it your best?" President Carter thought for a moment and said, "No, I haven't." The sergeant shot back, "Carter, why not the best?"

Why not the best? If anything is worth doing, it is worth giving our best. In our service to the Lord and others, we ought to be not only servantlike but sacrificial, willing, and selfless as well.

Willing to give everything he had for the Lord, the apostle Paul basically said in 2 Timothy 4:6, "I'm poured out like a drink offering. I have given everything. I have offered up everything in service to the Lord."

In order to serve effectively, the cupbearer had to offer the full cup, but he had to be like a vessel that was full and empty at the same time. In the same way, you should be full enough so that you don't need compliments or accolades to do your job, but empty enough so that you can be poured into, or trusted. Nehemiah was trustworthy in that he was always willing to be trusted by the king and selfless for the king's sake.

Notice that Jesus was also empty and full at the same time. The ultimate Nehemiah was a model cupbearer, but the greatest cupbearer was not Nehemiah—it was Jesus. In the Garden of Gethsemane He prayed, "Lord, let this cup pass from Me," yet this Cupbearer became a cross-bearer and exchanged the cup for a cross. He went to Calvary and died for the sins of the world. May we be like Jesus Christ, the ultimate Cupbearer, who exchanged His cup for a cross in total sacrifice. As the old hymn says, "Must Jesus bear the cross alone and all the world go free? No, there's a cross for everyone, and there's a cross for me." §

Chapter 3

The Heart of the King

(Nehemiah 2:2-10)

Proverbs 21:1 lets us know that the heart of the king is in the hand of the Lord, and like a river He moves it in whatever direction He chooses. It is so important to know that when we approach the kingdoms of this world, whether they are political, financial, social, or academic, the heart of the king on earth is controlled by the King in heaven. Sometimes God can influence a king to be hard and harsh, as in Exodus 7:3, when He said to Moses, "I will harden Pharaoh's heart." But just as God can harden the heart of the king, He can also soften it. God's hand is in control. As the psalmist says, "[We] should look unto the hills from which cometh [our] help, knowing that [our] help cometh from the Lord" (Psalm 121:1 KJV).

This principle is illustrated through the life of Nehemiah. Nehemiah had been weeping and praying over the ruins of Jerusalem. Yet God led him to a program of recovery. This passage of Scripture wonderfully illustrates how the damaged and ruined areas of our lives can be rebuilt. So many people are rebuilding their physical lives after tragedy and trouble, such as the victims hit by Hurricane Sandy. Yet certain emotional and spiritual areas in *all* of our lives need to be repaired, recovered, and restored too. As we explore the work and life of Nehemiah, we shall find practical help to reclaim and restore those ruined areas.

In chapter 2, Nehemiah was preparing to make his petition to King Artaxerxes. An opportunity had arisen rather unexpectedly for Nehemiah to approach the king with a petition to allow him to take a leave of absence to help rebuild the walls of Jerusalem.

Notice the perspective of the king. In the Book of Ezra, the same Artaxerxes allowed Ezra and his fellow priests to return to Jerusalem after living under reproach in Babylon. Even though the Persian king did not believe in Yahweh, he still gave them permission to return to Jerusalem, even supplying them with ample provisions for their journey. Artaxerxes was a pagan king with a compassionate heart. The same God who moved on the heart of the king to allow him to give permission and possessions to Ezra was able to do it through Nehemiah as well.

When the favor and fruit of God is in your life, He will bless you from unexpected places. It is no secret what God can do. He blesses your neighbor, and He can bless you too.

Verse 6 says that the queen was sitting next to the king. (This detail was deliberately placed in the text, not included by accident.) Some Bible scholars think this queen might have been Esther because she was Jewish and thus would be interested in restoring Jerusalem. Other scholars disagree, saying that Artaxerxes' reign came before that time, even though Esther may have been the mother-in-law of the queen mentioned here. But whatever the situation actually was, there was at least a likelihood that Esther had some influence on this queen and king.

In the same way, when God gives you an advantage, you should use it to promote others. Dr. E. K. Bailey, the late pastor of the Concord Missionary Baptist Church in Dallas, once said that when God gives you an advantage, you should use your advantage for the disadvantaged.

Notice that this chapter has a different date and opening words from chapter 1, which took place in Chislev, approximately the same month as our present-day December. Now, Nisan, mentioned at the beginning of chapter 2, directly corresponds to our month of April. This indicates a lapse of approximately four months.

It was in the month of Nisan on the Hebrew calendar when Nehemiah finally got an opportunity to inform the king about his concern for Jerusalem. We're not told why Nehemiah delayed that long before bringing this problem to the king, but we can presume that because he was a man of prayer, he was waiting for the Lord to indicate the right time. Suddenly, in the month of Nisan that time had come.

God often works that way in our lives. We sometimes are hasty, impatient creatures who want what we want when we want it. We want our prayers answered tomorrow—or even yesterday. We pray and expect God to answer right away, but often God delays His answers. It's not because He isn't powerful or willing to do what we ask. Many passages in the Scriptures teach us that a delayed answer doesn't indicate God is unwilling. We are exhorted again and again in the Bible to persevere and keep praying. Jesus said in the Sermon on the Mount, "Ask and it will be given; seek, and you shall find; knock, and the door will be opened" (Matthew 7:7 NKJV).

It's important to wait on the timing of God. If Nehemiah had rushed in, he would have been so emotional and impractical that he would have forfeited the rebuilding of the project—and possibly lost his own life. Many of us rush into things that we're unprepared for and wind up stepping ahead of God and making horrible mistakes. For example, many desire to be married, yet they are not ready emotionally, spiritually, and financially. Indeed, it does take more than love to pay the bills.

While Nehemiah was waiting, he was preparing so

that when the opportunity did come, he would be ready. He had thought out his goal clearly, along with the ways to accomplish it. He was praying and preparing for what he needed.

Are you praying? Are you prepared? In Shakespeare's *Julius Caesar*, Brutus says to Cassius, "There is a tide in the affairs of men. Which, taken at the flood, leads on to fortune." Blacksmiths used to say, "Strike while the iron is hot." Famed American bandleader Les Brown said, "It is better to be prepared for an opportunity and not have one than to have an opportunity and not be prepared." What is it that you are desiring? What is it that you want? If the opportunity came today, would you really be prepared for it? Would you be ready to move, or to shift? Do you have the skills, the abilities, and the know-how to step into that opportunity?

Nehemiah had been so troubled over the state of Jerusalem that when he came before the king while performing his normal duties, his face showed concern. This was the first time he had ever appeared in such a melancholy state, but apparently his concern was so great that it broke through on his face. The king noticed this immediately and asked him, "Why are you so sad?" Nehemiah tells us that his response to the question was fear. He was afraid because monarchs in that day believed their very presence brought joy and happiness, so at that moment Nehemiah could have lost his life for being sad in front of the king.

Therefore, Nehemiah's fear had a sound basis. Remember that he was a cupbearer. It was his responsibility to taste the king's wine before it was served to make sure that no one could poison him. The usual method involved poisoning his food or wine. This was a dangerous job Nehemiah had. It's obvious that he was a man of unlimited integrity and trustworthiness whom the king trusted explicitly. If the king ever grew suspicious or distrustful of him, Nehemiah's life would be in danger, so he prayed. When he was asked that question, he took a few seconds to pray for wisdom.

Nehemiah immediately sensed this was a moment of danger, but it was also a moment when God was opening a door. So Nehemiah's response was to shoot up a quick prayer—e-mailing, faxing, or texting a prayer, if you will, to God. In his thoughts, without words, he formulated a quick plea for help before he made his response. (Many of us would do well to send up a prayer to God before responding to some things—before taking that test, before attending that meeting, before going to work, or before facing the next challenge.) Nehemiah prayed nine times in thirteen chapters. Usually they were short prayers.

But it's not how long you pray; it's *how well* you pray.

Sometimes all you can say is, "Lord, have mercy," but that's enough of a prayer to impact critical situations and allow God to deliver you and give you refuge.

There's a story about Justice and Mercy, who were planning a meeting to decide the fate of the world. Just like it always happened, Justice was on time, but Mercy was late. When Mercy got there, his clothes were wet and soot covered his torn clothes. Justice said, "Mercy, you were supposed to be here two hours ago. You're late! And look, you're not even dressed appropriately for the meeting."

Mercy said, "I would have been on time, but while I was on my way, I stopped by the Red Sea. I saw Moses and the children of Israel and their enemies behind them. I heard Moses cry, 'Lord, have mercy,' so I had to get into the Red Sea and divide it. That's why I'm wet. I still could have made it, but then I stopped by a fiery furnace with Shadrach, Meshach, and Abednego inside. I had to get into the fire and control the heat. That's why there's soot on my clothes. I could have made it on time, but I stopped by and saw Daniel in the lions' den. I heard him cry out, 'Lord, have mercy.' I had to get into the lions' den and close the mouths of the lions. So that's why my clothes are torn up. In fact, Justice, I gotta go now because I hear somebody else saying, 'Lord, have mercy.' "

Notice Nehemiah's plea before the king, which included requests for leave, letters, and lumber. First of all, he asked for a leave of absence. He originally said that he needed leave for a few days or five months, but he was actually gone for twelve years. Yet he still had responsibly asked the king for leave from his job. Nehemiah also asked for letters because he had to travel eight hundred miles from Persia to Jerusalem. He would have to travel through foreign nations, and the kings and governors who didn't know him might have tried to do him harm. So, he had to be prepared to show them a letter to allow him to pass through their various provinces. Finally, Nehemiah requested enough lumber to build the walls, along with a home while he was gone.

In verse 8 Nehemiah received everything from the king that he asked for. Verses 2, 10, and 18 refer to "the hand of the Lord." The hand of the Lord will give you favor; this speaks of the gracious blessing of God, which includes the fuel—His providence and provision. Notice that the king provided Nehemiah with a military escort that he didn't even ask for. When the hand of the Lord is on your life, God will give you "good measure, pressed down, shaken together, and running over" (Luke 6:38 NKJV). He will bless you exceedingly, abundantly above all that you can ask or think (Ephesians 3:20).

Notice in verses 9 and 10, however, that favor also brings foes. Nehemiah was met by two very troublesome enemies when he got there: Sanballat the Horonite and Tobiah the Ammonite. A Horonite was devoted to the god of Horon, the local deity of Palestine. This indicates that he was a pagan. Tobiah was a citizen of Ammon, which was the country that is now called Jordan, whose present-day capital is Amman. Ammon, one of the tribes descended from Lot, the nephew of Abraham, was related to the children of Israel. Yet Ammon always was an enemy of Israel.

Favor will draw enemies to you, but they cannot stop the ongoing plan of God in your life. God is still in control. He is still demonstrating that He can work in your life.

Nehemiah said, "So I went to Jerusalem . . ." In other words, in spite of the enemies, in spite of those who meant him harm, in spite of his haters, he kept going.

Likewise, don't let haters stop you from fulfilling what God has for you. First John 4:4 (NKJV) says, "You are of God, little children, and have overcome them, because He who is in you is greater than he who is in the world." Continue to walk in the favor of God, knowing that the hand of the King in heaven controls the heart of the king on earth. §

Chapter 4

You've Got To Face It To Fix It

(Nehemiah 2:11-20)

Nehemiah spearheaded the building project because he had the heart of a leader. He had inquired about the people, internalized the pain, interceded through prayer, and implored a potentate. Then he investigated the predicament. In order to repair the broken walls, he had to make an assessment of the damages. He had to face the problem in order to fix it.

So it is with us as we are repairing and rebuilding broken areas in our lives; we must face and assess the damages—the ramifications of our ruined areas—before we can make a repair. God shows us through the life of Nehemiah how to face the broken areas of our condition, as well as prepare to fix them.

Nehemiah examined the problem. Nehemiah had spent time with God in silence and solitude, and this is what prepared him for the public stage.

Similarly, those periods of anonymity spent with God in prayer and times of preparation propel us to the public stage. If we are faithful over a few things, in God's own time, He will take us from the background to the forefront—from anonymity to celebrity.

In her book, *Anonymous: Jesus' Hidden Years . . . and Yours*, Alicia Britt Chole acknowledges that of Jesus' thirty-three years on earth, thirty were—for the most part—hidden from the public. He was actually in the public ministry for only three years. He lived ninety percent of His life in anonymity and only ten percent in public. Yet it is what Jesus did in private that gave significance and power to what He was able to do in public.

So many of us rush to get on the stage, but if we do not handle the time of privacy correctly, it can have a negative impact when we're in public. While he was in private, Nehemiah was surveying the situation. Nehemiah did not go to Jerusalem with a bunch of fanfare. Instead, he only told a few people about it. He did not share his views publicly.

Verse 13 says Nehemiah "examined" the wall. The word in Hebrew suggests the idea of a doctor probing a wound before he gives a diagnosis. And while he was examining the walls and the various gates, he discovered that the problem was actually worse than he had anticipated. Apparently the walls were in such a state of ruin and cluttered with so much rubble and debris that his horse couldn't even pass through. But Nehemiah analyzed the problem and did not assume anything. Instead, he acknowledged the problem, which propelled and prepared him to rebuild the wall.

This is much like someone who has an addiction. They must admit and face the fact of their addiction before they can ever begin to recover.

Nehemiah personally explored the extent of his problem, and then he informed the ones who must do the work. This was definitely a moment of challenge, when Nehemiah began to involve others in the work. According to verse 17 he reported the condition of the wall. This is a wonderful example of good leadership. He couldn't do the work alone, so he had to involve others.

So Nehemiah appealed to their pride. He said, "You can see the ruins around you." He further pointed out that for a hundred years the wall had been down, and it was a sign and symbol of disgrace. Yet it was really a sign reflecting a deeper leadership problem—what was going on physically with the walls represented what was going on spiritually among the people. The reason why the walls had not been rebuilt was because the leadership did not rise up.

In his book, *The 21 Irrefutable Laws of Leadership*, John C. Maxwell says the first law is called the law of the lid. He says that leadership ability determines the level of effectiveness of any organization. In other words, you do not have a "9" or "10" organization when you have a "4" or "5" leader. This is true of any church ministry, government agency, school, business, or even a sports team. Everything rises and falls on leadership.

The wall was down for a hundred and twenty years, but it was rebuilt in fifty-two days. Why? Because a leader showed up. Nothing happens until a leader shows up. God calls us to be like Nehemiah—to lift the lid and raise the consciousness of people so that they can see their potential and then reach it.

Then Nehemiah made a recommendation. He put it to them plainly that it was time to act. He said that God had already helped by moving the heart of the king to give leave, labor, and lumber to him.

Now it was time to rebuild. Nehemiah galvanized the Jews to action, so they began the process of rebuilding. At first he said, "Let's rise up and build," but then there was a transfer of passion—from Nehemiah to the people. In verse 19, they said, "Let's rise up and build." §

Chapter 5

Get In Where You Fit In

(Nehemiah 3)

For want of a nail the shoe was lost.
For want of a shoe the horse was lost.
For want of a horse the rider was lost.
For want of a rider the message was lost.
For want of a message the battle was lost.
For want of a battle the kingdom was lost.

Everyone has a part to play and a place to stand when it comes to the work of the Lord. There is no place for spectators and self-appointed advisors and critics, but there's always room for workers. As we study Nehemiah 3, we discover the principles that apply to leadership and labor, as well as loving the work and projects of the Lord. Notice that the purpose of the Hebrews' work was to glorify God.

Nehemiah was concerned about one thing: the glory of God. He said, "Let us rise up and build the wall of Jerusalem that there be no reproach" for there was much mocking and ridicule of the Jews because the wall was down. The purpose for rebuilding the wall was to glorify God, but also to protect the people doing the rebuilding. The setting of the gates also was meant for the protection and security of the people. Jerusalem was surrounded by enemies, so it seemed foolish for the residents to improve the inside but have nothing to protect it because they would be at risk. When Nehemiah arrived on the scene, he challenged them to rebuild the city to the glory of God.

Nehemiah was a leader who planned his work and worked his plan. The way he led the people in this project is an example for us to follow. With Nehemiah's plan, everyone had a place.

In 1 Corinthians 12:14, Paul compares individual Christians to members of the human body. Each member is important, and each has a specific part to play. One person cannot and does not do everything.

I recall the time in my own pastoral ministry at Metropolitan New Testament Mission Baptist Church when I was relieved to discover that God did not expect me to do everything, whether it was in the area of ministry or missions. God had sent and would continue to send gifted people who would help as they were trained and equipped for the work of the ministry. We would encourage them to discover, develop, and then demonstrate their own gifts in accomplishing the work of the Lord. This was greatly demonstrated in the building of our church edifice—a 19,000 square-foot church building that includes a sanctuary, classrooms, and offices. It was not built by one person, but by everyone pooling their resources together, utilizing their God-given gifts to construct a building to the glory of God.

Notice that the involvement of the people starts with the leaders because leaders always set the example. The city leaders essentially took this layman Nehemiah, who began working, but the actual labor for the project transferred from the leaders to the people.

Verse 2 says that some of the builders came from the city of Jericho. Jericho was famous for having wall problems. But when they came from Jericho, they had to cross ethnic lines to join with the Jewish people of Jerusalem in order to rebuild the walls. In other words, they had to take the road from Jericho to Jerusalem. Similarly, to build a great church you must have people who are willing to cross all the lines—racial, economic, and educational.

At the Metropolitan Church where I serve, we have racial, economic, and educational diversity. I always say we are like alphabet soup. We have Ph.Ds sitting right next to ABCs, and beauticians sitting right next to morticians. It is beautiful because, as the song says, "Red, yellow, black, and white/We are precious in God's sight."

Verse 8 says that the goldsmiths and the perfumers were on hand to help build the wall. They were considered different because they dealt with gold jewelry and little, tiny, microscopic, flowery things, but that also was important. They had to risk doing something that had never been done before. In the same way, to build a great ministry, project, or business, you have to risk doing something that's never been done before.

Notice in verse 5 that there were those who were not committed to the work. It says that there was a group that would not "put their necks to the work of the Lord" (KJV). That phrase literally means that they were stubborn. In other words, they refused to help.

This was a different experience for Nehemiah because up to this point things had been rather smooth for him. He had been successful with the king in that he had been granted all that he asked for. Even the people and the other leaders agreed to help him rebuild the wall. His enemies had been kept at bay, but now there was a group that refused to submit to authority and help build the wall. The Modern Language Bible says that "they did not condescend to serve the Lord." In other words, they did not humble themselves.

It's important to realize that everyone will not participate or support the work of the Lord. They are too myopic in their mentality, too puny in their perception, too satanic in their sight, and too devilish in their dealings. But notice that Nehemiah did not beg or implore them to help. He just continued to do what he did. Likewise, you can't help it if people won't support what you're doing, nor can you allow the work to be held up by a few people who don't catch the vision.

The people worked in several places at the gate in order to finish the work. There were some who worked at the Old Gate (v. 6). Some worked at the New Gate, but there were others who still had to work at the Old Gate.

The church does not continue by being based on new and exciting areas of ministry. It's the people committed to the old gate who are essential to the church's survival. The old gate is represented by the people who open the doors of the church, take care of the babies, hand out the bulletins, and a lot of other stuff that happens in church. Those people are willing to come back and serve Sunday after Sunday, week after week, month after month, year after year at the old gate, doing the same things that generations of people have done. Many people don't understand that about church life. They think that everything in church needs to be new and exciting, but you can't have an effective church without people who are committed to the old gate.

Verse 14 says that some of the people worked at the Dung Gate. You don't need a Ph.D in Hebrew to know that this gate was not a very pleasant place. The Dung Gate was a place filled with ruminating animals such as donkeys, horses, camels, and goats—all producing dung. It was an awful, hard place. Today, for some of us working to reach the city of Christ, we've got to work at the dung gate. We've got to deal with unpleasant people and situations to accomplish the work of the Lord.

There were others who worked at the Water Gate (v. 26). In chapter 8, we learn that this was the location where Ezra read the Law—where the Word of God was revered and respected. In Scripture, water is a symbol of the Word of God because it has cleansing power. Ephesians 5:26 says that we're cleansed by the washing of the Word. So we need the Word of God. Interestingly, this was the only gate that did not need to be repaired. Similarly, the Word of God never needs improvement because it will last forever. "The flower fadeth, the grass withereth, but the word of God shall stand forever" (Isaiah 40:8 KJV).

Verses 1 and 32 refer to the Sheep Gate, where the work began and ended. This is the gate of sacrifice, for in the work of the Lord we must sacrifice. Paul says, "I die daily" (1 Corinthians 15:31 NKJV). The most interesting thing is that the people rebuilt the walls, never knowing who would walk through them.

I believe that we should plant trees we will not eat from, but generations yet unborn will benefit from. Wise people build shade trees they will never sit under. Who knows which child running around the church walls today will someday make their mark in the world and go forward, beyond those very walls? Yet they will always have those walls to look back on that shaped them and began to develop their character.

Who would have thought in that church in Detroit, Michigan, where Ben Carson grew up running around its walls, that one day he would grow up and become the head of pediatric neurosurgery at Johns Hopkins Hospital, where he would lead a surgical team of seventy to operate for twenty-two hours and use his gifted hands to separate the Binder twins in 1987? People built that church in Detroit, Michigan, where he grew up. Ben Carson was running around those walls, and no one knew even then that those gifted hands would somehow save lives.

Who would've guessed that in the New Hope Baptist Church in Newark, New Jersey, a girl would sing her first solo in the choir that her mother directed, and her gift would be so powerful that a record producer, Clive Davis, would hear her and want to give her a record contract? Who would have thought that she would sell over two hundred million records and videos and she would become the most awarded and celebrated female musical act in history?

Who would have thought that a boy running around the Ebenezer Baptist Church in Atlanta, Georgia, would someday leave that church and go on to Morehouse

College at the age of fifteen, lead a bus boycott in Montgomery, Alabama, give one of the most famous speeches in history, receive the Nobel Peace Prize, and now has a monument dedicated to his honor in Washington, D.C., next to the Lincoln, Jefferson, and Washington Memorials? That young boy running around that church was Dr. Martin Luther King, Jr.

Why build this particular wall in Jerusalem? People built the wall, and after they died, their bodies were buried and turned to dust, while their souls rested in the bosom of Abraham. The wall stood there and held together in the City of David. It stood there throughout the reign of Alexander the Great, who conquered the city in 332 B.C. It stayed there throughout the time of the Maccabees, who took the city back in 166 B.C.

Years later, at that same wall a twelve-year-old boy came to that sheep gate with His mother and father. After leaving the city, His parents couldn't find Him for a while, even though they searched for Him everywhere. Finally when they found Him, He said, "I must be about my Father's business." Twenty years later He rode through those same city gates on Palm Sunday. On that one day He was given the honor He so richly deserved, but a few days later they took Him back through those gates on that Good Friday and led Him to a hill called Calvary where He died on the cross. They pierced Him in the side and put Him in a tomb. He rose from the dead, and He's coming back again. So, continue to work for God because you never know what benefit your work and building will have. §

Chapter 6

Building and Battling

(Nehemiah 4)

There was a casualty during the eight days of conflict between Israel and the militant group Hamas in the Gaza Strip in 2011. Salem Boulos Sweilem, a member of the Gaza Baptist Church in the Gaza Strip and the father of five, worked in the city as a carpenter. On the night of November 19th Israeli war planes dropped bombs nearby at Palestine Stadium, and the subsequent blast caused Salam's building to shake. When he awoke, he panicked because he couldn't breathe. His family wanted to take him to a hospital but had no transportation. They finally found a neighbor with a car, but by then it was too late. He died while on his way to the hospital.

It seems like everything new is old again. The sons and daughters of Isaac and Ishmael are still involved in the same endless battle that they were engaged in twenty-four hundred years ago. The conflict between Jews and Arabs is still prevalent.

While the Jews were working on the wall in the fourth chapter, local opposition threatened them, planning to fight against them. Enemies rose up in the name of Sanballat, Tobiah, and Geshem, ancient enemies of the people of God. Their negativity discouraged even the workers who had started building, but one man, their leader Nehemiah, stood up and said, "Stop being afraid and remember God." The opposition vanished, and they continued to build—with a sword in one hand and a trowel in the other.

If you're doing a great and progressive work for God, you will face opposition. But a visionary leader can overcome it and rally the people to finish the work of the Lord. How does this happen?

It comes by first understanding that a progressive work for God will inevitably face opposition. Verses 1 through 5 basically say that whenever there is progress being made, there will inevitably be sideline scorners and sidewalk critics. When the people of God say, "Let's rise up and build," Satan says, "Let's rise up and battle." The Enemy will always assign someone to divert you from the purposeful plan of God for your life. The only way to not have a critic is to have nothing, do nothing, and be about nothing, because nothing from nothing leaves nothing.

In this chapter, there indeed was a plot of the enemy. Sanballat, Tobiah, and Geshem were paranoid that the Jews would in some kind of way hurt them. So they began to be patronizing towards the work with diversion, distraction, and discouragement. And they predicted that the project would fail and not succeed. So Nehemiah quickly said a prayer of victory.

Prayer is the steering wheel, not the spare tire, in the life of the believer. Prayer is a privilege of the believer. Although we are quick to retaliate, we need to respond initially through prayer. We need to take opposition to a higher level in prayer.

This reminds me of a story about a flight attendant sitting in the back of a plane. As the plane is getting ready to take off, she calls the cockpit to alert the pilot that there's a snake on the plane. The pilot tells the flight attendant to stay calm—that everything's okay. She calls back and says, "It's not okay. There's a snake on the plane. I don't know if it's poisonous or not, but you need to do something." She calls back, noticing that the plane has begun to taxi down the runway. She says, "Are you taking this plane up in the air?" He says, "Just stay calm; stay reserved." They fly up to fifteen thousand feet, twenty thousand feet, and then twenty-five thousand feet. He calls back to the flight attendant and says, "How's the snake?" She says, "It appears to be dead." When the plane lands and they reach their destination, she asks the pilot, "How did you know to do that? Why did you keep going?" He replies, "Snakes are subterranean and cannot exist in elevated levels. So I took it to such an elevation that it could not survive."

When there are snakes on your job, snakes in your home, and even snakes in your church, you need to take it up to a higher level in prayer. Take it up in fasting and worship, and the snakes will be destroyed.

Verses 10 through 14 indicate that those who are involved in the work can be discouraged. They get discouraged and begin to believe what the Enemy is saying. If the Enemy can get in your head, he can make you believe you're defeated before the fight even starts. In this chapter Judah rose up and repeated what their enemies said—that they would not succeed. They were intimidated! In the same way, if you're not careful, Satan can get into your mind so effectively that you can believe you won't succeed, you can't graduate, your child can't learn, you'll always be in debt, or you and your family will never be reconciled.

In Numbers 13:33 ten spies came back with a negative report, saying, "We were grasshoppers in their sight." How did they know they were grasshoppers? Because they were grasshoppers in their own sight! In his epic work *Paradise Lost,* renowned poet John Milton said that "the mind is its own place and in itself can make a heaven of hell, a hell of heaven."

When Nehemiah saw their fear, as a leader he rose up and told them not to fear. First of all, he said to them, "Don't fear, remember God, and fight for your family." "Fear not" was what he said! I do not think it's by accident that there are 365 "fear not's" in the King James Version of the Bible and 365 days in our calendar year. It's as if God's saying, "For every day that you wake up, I'm giving you a 'fear not.' " God does not want us to spend even one day in fear. Life is filled with battles, so we must battle even when we're building. But while rebuilding the ruined places of our lives, we are not supposed to fear because God is with us, and He will strengthen us to win every battle and conquer the Enemy. §

Chapter 7

Man in the Mirror

(Nehemiah 5)

Mirrors are marvelous contraptions, ever since Narcissus fell in love with his own image while gazing into a pond. The human race has always been fascinated by mirrors. Mirrors are the friends of magicians and the enemies of aging celebrities. We have round mirrors, square mirrors, big mirrors, compact mirrors, bathroom mirrors, and rearview mirrors. What greater vanity can be expressed than that of the Wicked Witch and Snow White, who asked their mirrors, "Mirror, mirror on the wall, who's the fairest of them all?" The mirror was tiny Alice's magical vehicle through which she could pass into Wonderland, the land of enchantment.

For the apostle Paul, the mirror symbolized a dim understanding of the mysterious things of God. He said in 1 Corinthians 13:12 (KJV), "For now we see through a glass, darkly; but then face to face: now I know in part; but then shall I know even as also I am known."

The mirror is also a starting point for change and transition. We will discover that the initial part and point of change is recognizing the change and then being the change that we desire. In those we lead and influence in the community and our homes, it all starts with the man or woman in the mirror. Mahatma Gandhi said, "We must be a part of the change that we want to see." President Obama said in his 2008 campaign, "We are the change that we seek."

Nehemiah demonstrated this principle in chapter 5 when God was restoring the people of Israel. The walls were being rebuilt and the gates repaired. He had already addressed the enemies from without, yet now he had to deal with the unrest within his own ranks.

During difficult times some of the wealthier Jews had loaned money to the poorer Jews. The problem was usury, charging interest for money that had been loaned. This was a practice that wasn't allowed for Jews to do to their own race. The Law prohibited them from charging interest to their own brother. In Exodus 22:25 (NKJV) Moses said, "If you lend money to *any of* My people *who are* poor among you, you shall not be like a moneylender to him; you shall not charge him." A Jew was supposed to loan the money as if he were loaning it to a brother—without interest. Verse 11 tells us what the interest rate was—one hundredth part per month, which would be one percent of the total or twelve percent per year. This does not sound as excessive as the eighteen percent we pay for credit card debt, but it was enough to outrage Nehemiah. (The loan sharks were at work even in those days.) When the poor people could not repay the loan, their properties were repossessed, and they became slaves of the wealthy Jews.

Nehemiah responded to this exploitation with a powerful example of integrity. At a public hearing, he stood up and rebuked them for usury, exhorting them not only to stop the practice but also insisting that they pay back what they had gotten unjustly. Their reaction in verse 12 was surprising: they willingly did it, not only because Nehemiah demanded it, but because of his example.

If Nehemiah had been corrupt in verse 12, that response on their part to change would never had happened. Likewise, it is our example that gives us the spiritual and moral authority to correct those who engage in exploitation. No man with an experience is at the mercy of a man with an argument. Nehemiah offered up his own experience, which was demonstrated first of all by what he did not do. He had already demonstrated his own integrity and transparency by not using his position to get rich or enhance his lifestyle as some officials had done to advance their lavish lifestyles. He had every right as the governor to take a salary and demand certain things. But Nehemiah said, "I did not do that."

Second, he often fed the hundred and fifty officials

with feasts at his own expense. What a remarkable picture of concern and compassion! Nehemiah did this in part because he certainly had his own personal wealth as a cupbearer. But just because people have wealth doesn't mean they will share it. Nehemiah, however, was willing to sacrifice his wants and even allowed them to eat at his own table the food prepared for himself. He understood the principle Jesus taught His disciples in Matthew 10:8 (NKJV): "Freely you have received, freely give."

The fact of the matter is that leadership has no answer to exploitation unless it can point to its own integrity. It is our example of integrity—the change in the man or woman in the mirror—that gives us the spiritual and moral authority to expect that in other people.

The reason why some children don't value the opinions of their parents is because their parents don't walk in integrity. Children are experts at detecting hypocrisy; all they have to do is watch. Many of us want to act any way in front of our unsaved friends and family and then invite them to church.

At some point, however, the gospel must change us. At some point we have to say with the apostle Paul, "Follow me as I follow Christ" (1 Corinthians 11:1). We can never expect people to rise higher than our own leadership, any more than a boat can rise higher than the water it's placed in. People can never rise higher than the one leading them.

The people were able to receive Nehemiah's instruction due to his tremendous example. He became the change he desired to see in others. Likewise, in order to effectuate real change in others, we must become the change that we seek. We must first change the man or woman in the mirror. How do we become the change that we seek in others?

We all have gifts, talents, and abilities, unless we are just pathological or incurable. Everyone has some good gift and ought to use it as a resource for God's kingdom. The real acid test is what we're doing for God, even if there is absolutely no gain to be received for it—no applause, no recognition, no accolades, no announcements, no pronouncements, and no financial compensation.

There's a story about Mother Teresa, who was ministering in a leper colony in the Village of Calcutta. A tour group was visiting there while Mother Teresa was cleaning the wound of a leper. When the tourists saw that, under their breath they said, "I wouldn't do that for a million dollars." Without even looking up, Mother Teresa replied, "I wouldn't either." In other words, she was saying that what God has given us, we should freely share for the sake of His kingdom.

So, this deplorable practice of exploitation that existed amongst the Jews was successfully handled by Nehemiah. Later in chapter 5, the unseen enemy tried yet another approach, internal strife, which was no longer an attack from without, but within. This is the only chapter in which no building was taking place. Nehemiah stopped the building to deal with internal issues.

There were many complaints from the people about these city officials while they were working on this wall day and night. They had no time to plant crops, yet they had to eat. They had to pay taxes (vv. 4-5). In those days, if you couldn't pay your taxes or your debt, you were sold into slavery. Your children and wives were slaves until you paid back what you owed. This had already happened to some of them by verse 5. Nehemiah dealt with this issue earnestly and forthrightly.

This practice of exploitation is among us even today. Some will misuse and abuse, exploit and even pervert the opportunity for restoration. There always will be exploitation because it's just a fact of human existence. The very moment we got the Internet, we had Internet crime. Most recently, Facebook had to shut down a recruiting page for the Pakistani Taliban that was designed to connect with people around the world.

There will always be those who seek to pervert that

which is good. Recently in Youngstown, Ohio, a Scrooge apparently dressed as a Salvation Army employee stole all the hundreds of pennies, nickels, dimes, and dollars collected for the less fortunate from a red kettle of the Salvation Army that's found in front of many malls and stores during Christmastime. The theft was all captured on surveillance camera. The man brought back the money with a letter of apology, feeling guilty for what he had done. The real issue is that we are living in a day when a person with that type of tender conscience is so rare that when he has a change of heart and demonstrates some values, it makes national news.

Verses 13 through 19 indicate that the ultimate test of all authority and righteous judgment is God. Ultimately God is the only real guarantor of integrity. When Nehemiah shook his garment (v. 13), he was actually saying that God would shake them out if they didn't keep their promise not to exploit the people. They understood exactly what that meant. In the Old Testament this symbolic gesture belonged to a species of action that demonstrated and articulated what God was going to do.

It's the same type of symbolic action presented in the battle of Ai (Joshua 8:18). When Joshua pointed the spear in a certain way, God was going to give them the victory over Ai. Also, in 2 Kings 13:15-19, when Elijah put his hand on the king's hands and shot the arrow out the window towards the Syrians, it was a way of articulating that God was going to move against them on their behalf.

In verse 19 Nehemiah prayed to God as if recognizing that He could see the intent of their hearts. He was really saying, "Of everyone, including me and you, God is the ultimate judge." It was a prophecy to Israel that both illustrated and commended God's action toward them.

Some people seem like the ones who can fool all the people some of the time. Some people can fool some of the people all the time. Some people are so good that they can fool all the people all the time, but you can't fool God any of the time. God will unmask all that's hidden. Proverbs 15:3 (KJV) says, "The Lord's eyes are in every place, beholding the evil and the good." Our sins will find us out. So our prayer needs to be the prayer of Psalm 139: "Search me and try me. And if You find anything that's not like You, TAKE IT OUT!" §

Chapter 8

"I Cannot Come Down"

(Nehemiah 6)

The Agony and the Ecstasy is a great movie about the relationship between Michelangelo, played by Charlton Heston, and Pope Julio II, played by Rex Harrison. There's a famous scene with Pope Julio standing on the floor of the Sistine Chapel, trying to get Michelangelo to come down. Yet the great artist would not come down before finishing his project of painting the ceiling of the famous chapel. Instead, he stays upon the scaffold. Even when the scaffold collapses, he still would not come down.

More recently, the Rev. Corey Brooks, pastor of the New Beginning Church of Chicago, Illinois, was determined to see his community transformed. He had been asking the city to tear down the motel across the street from his church because it had a reputation for crime, especially drugs and prostitution. He was so determined to see this South Side motel torn down and a community center be built in its place that he camped on a roof of the motel for ninety-four days through the winter season and would not come down. City officials, civic leaders, and even some religious leaders in the city thought he was crazy for doing this and told him to come down. He garnered so much media attention that the actor and movie producer Tyler Perry donated a hundred thousand dollars to his cause. After that contribution was made, a local businessman anonymously donated $85,000, and that was enough to tear down the crime-ridden motel and begin a fundraising campaign for the community center.

In chapter 6 of this biblical story, Nehemiah had been building the wall in Jerusalem, which represented the protection and provision of God. He was near the completion of the project when Sanballat and Geshem attempted to meet with Nehemiah four times so they could harm him. Realizing their evil plot, Nehemiah refused each time, saying his work was too important to stop. Then Sanballat and Geshem showed Nehemiah a letter they had written to King Artaxerxes that claimed Nehemiah and the Jews planned to rebel. The enemy used a prophet named Shemaiah to try to persuade Nehemiah to seek refuge inside the temple. Nehemiah saw through that scheme to intimidate and discredit him, and he refused.

This passage shows us that anyone involved in a great and progressive work for God will be tempted at some point to cease from the labor. We must be determined, however, not to stop; indeed, we must not come down. Like Nehemiah, all of us, whatever our vocations may be, are building something—a marriage, family, career, business, legacy, ministry, or community. If we are in any sense constructing something great and progressive, if we've climbed up on anything in life to build something constructive, we can be sure that there will be those who will want to pull us down. But we cannot succumb to that temptation, that trap, or trick. Each one of us must be determined not to cease from doing what God wants us to do.

Anyone doing a great and progressive work for God will be tempted to come down due to opposition. One lesson that clearly emerges in the beginning of this book is that life is a battle from beginning to end.

Nehemiah ran into opposition the moment he set his heart to obey God's command to rebuild the walls and gates of Jerusalem. He faced difficulty before he even got to the city. And after he reached Jerusalem, enemies rose up to oppose everything that he did.

You may not have experienced all that in your Christian life, but you will. The apostle Paul warns us in Ephesians 6:12 (KJV) that our struggle is not against flesh and blood (men and women). What we are up against are invisible forces, or "rulers of darkness of this world," as Paul calls it.

Those same enemies found in the Book of Nehemiah

tried to deter his plan and progress. In the same way, we are confronted with enemies who hate law and order, along with justice and peace, and seek to bring down any progressive work of God. In 1 Corinthians 16:8-9 (ESV) the apostle Paul said, "A wide door for effective work is open to me, and there are many adversaries." Notice he mentioned "a wide door" and "many adversaries," meaning that the level and greatness of the opportunity will be matched with the intensity of opposition.

As 1 Peter 5:8 says, the Devil walks about like a roaring lion, seeking whom he may devour. A lion is a very dangerous, powerful, and fearsome enemy. In fact, it is so strong that one bite from his jaw can crush the thickest bone in a human body—the thigh bone. One blow from its mighty paw can smash a human skull like an eggshell. But the Devil has another capacity: this passage also reveals that he can come suddenly, without warning.

The Scriptures call the Devil an "angel of light" (2 Corinthians 11:14). He comes with smiling, gracious accommodations, enticing promises, and flattering words, assuring us that he means us no harm. But either route the Devil uses, whether it's fear or flattery, will end in our destruction. So we must guard ourselves against those approaches. Like the apostle Paul says in 2 Corinthians 2:11, we are not ignorant of Satan's devices.

Following a series of attacks and threats against him in an effort to intimidate Nehemiah from completing the wall, his enemies suddenly changed their tactics. Suddenly they resorted to friendliness and persuasion, but this tack was just as dangerous. The enemies suddenly wanted to become Nehemiah's friends and invited him to a conference down in the Plain of Ono. As we have already seen, these men had been Nehemiah's enemies, so he sensed danger. Verse 2 (KJV) says, "But they thought to do me mischief." The New International Version says, "They were scheming to harm me."

Some commentators suggest that they were trying to trick Nehemiah to leave Jerusalem, where he had armed support and armed guards, and come to a conference where they could attack him and perhaps even kill him while he was unprotected. Nehemiah evidently sensed this evil tactic and firmly declined, saying in verse 3, "I'm doing a great work and I cannot come down. Why should the work stop while I leave and come down to you?"

Nehemiah's answer, "I'm doing a great work," is a great one. We especially need to note this reason why he couldn't come, even though they tried inviting him four different times. One of the most helpful things that we can do to resist temptation is remember that

God has called us to a great task. This is true for every believer. It doesn't matter how young or how old you are; you are called to a great task.

In Jonathan Swift's novel *Gulliver's Travels*, Lemuel Gulliver ends up in a kingdom called Lilliput. This particular part of the book satirizes the kingdom of Great Britain. Gulliver finds himself tied down on a bench, unable to move. The Lilliputians have tied him down with little strings. The people, who are only six inches tall, make Gulliver their prisoner and take him into Lilliput. In the same way, if you're not careful, little people with little minds will try to pull you down from your great work, and soon you will be tied down with little things. Instead, you must be determined not to be strapped down by little, insignificant people or things because you're doing a great work.

Notice that Nehemiah asked them why the work should cease so he could come down. The project would be incomplete if he had come down. If he had left his calling, his work, or his post, it would have been unfinished. Coming down would have prevented him from completing what God wanted him to do.

There is nothing worse than unfinished work. In 2 Timothy 4:7 (KJV), Paul said, "I finished my course, I kept the faith." Jesus was able to say on the cross, "It is finished" (John 19:30). They were actually saying, "Lord, I've done everything that You told me to do." Nothing is worse than something unfinished.

In 1945 Elizabeth Shoumatoff painted an unfinished portrait of President Franklin D. Roosevelt. When she was beginning to paint the portrait, Roosevelt asked for a break. In the interim, Roosevelt died before she could complete the painting.

There's the Ryugyong Hotel in North Korea, an unfinished construction project. It was going to be the tallest hotel, as well as the seventh largest building, in the world, but they couldn't complete it because of structural issues. It is a monument to ineptitude. It's just standing there to this day because it's too costly to finish or tear down.

Franz Schubert is known for writing an unfinished symphony with only two pages left to finish the last movement.

But you'll want to be able to say at the end of your life that same statement the apostle Paul made, "I've finished the course, I've kept the faith. I've done whatever God has told me to do."

Anyone trying to accomplish a great, progressive work for God will also be tempted to come down though misrepresentation. When the Enemy cannot accomplish his purpose by offering peace and friendliness, he switches back to his original tactics of threats and danger.

His enemies had written a letter that suggested the Jews were going to revolt and Nehemiah would use this wall project for personal and political gain. It was a false accusation—a gross misrepresentation with a hidden motive. Notice in verse 5 that it was an unsealed letter. In other words, his enemies made sure that everyone involved with delivering the letter could read it and spread the lie that Nehemiah was trying to make himself king.

The misrepresentation and arm-twisting was designed to put pressure on Nehemiah to yield to their solicitation and thus fall into their trap. Yet he resisted because he saw the letter for what it really was—an enticement based upon lies, with no basis in fact. How did Nehemiah respond? He answered them with a flat denial. In verse 8 he said, "Nothing like what you're saying is happening." In other words, he told them that they were just making this up in their heads. Nehemiah responded to such charges in the right way, with just a flat denial. There was no attempt to disprove their accusation. He merely stressed that it was a lie and then moved on.

When you tell the truth, you never have to remember what you've said. The great thing about telling the truth is that it's the same anytime. The person who lies, however, has to go back and think back to what he said to this person or that person.

Don't be surprised if you're being misrepresented while doing the great work of God. Anyone who has ever done a progressive work for God will be misrepresented.

Joseph Kennedy, the patriarch of the Kennedy family, wheedled his way into the administration of President Franklin D. Roosevelt. He became the ambassador of Great Britain, the most prestigious ambassadorship of any kind. It was an extremely critical time. Adolf Hitler's power was expanding, and the world was teetering on the brink of World War II. Kennedy had the arrogance in 1938 to misrepresent the wishes of President Roosevelt and his cabinet to the British government. Kennedy had his own business and pacifist interests, so he acted as a free agent, misrepresenting the position and wishes of the President who had sent him there as his ambassador. Now, if it is unbelievable to think that an ambassador would misrepresent the intentions of a mere President, how much more could someone misrepresent the intentions and character of a man of God?

And yet in spite of misrepresentation, you must be determined not to come down from your wall. Anyone doing a great, progressive work for God must guard against the deceptive temptation to come down by using discernment.

Once again the enemies switched their tactics. In verse 10 this temptation for Nehemiah to come down came in the form of false prophecy. Shemaiah was a false prophet who claimed to have received a word for Nehemiah. He wanted Nehemiah to go with him into the inner chamber of the temple. Nehemiah detected that something was wrong because he knew that he wasn't permitted to go into the temple. Only the priests were allowed to enter in those days, and he was a layman. It was just a part of a plot to discredit him. Nehemiah used discernment and did not fall into the trap. As if he had a sixth sense, Nehemiah sniffed out this plot.

Those who do a great work for God must have a spirit of discernment. Discernment is the ability to perceive whether a person's actions originate from God, Satan, or mere human sources. There is a specific spiritual gift of discernment, according to 1 Corinthians 12:10, but then there is a certain level of discernment that all believers need to have, especially those engaged in a progressive work for the Lord.

The United States Army has what's called S-wave radar. Invented by the Massachusetts Institute of Technology (MIT), it's used in urban fighting in

Afghanistan. The last couple of years our soldiers fighting in Afghanistan have used it to fight from house to house. This specialized kind of radar can see through an eight-foot-thick wall at a distance of sixty feet and detect who is behind the wall, along with any activity. If MIT can come up with radar to detect what's behind a wall, how much more can the Spirit of God detect matters of the heart? We need our own spiritual wave radar that allows us to see through and discern the intent of one's heart. We need a spirit of discernment.

First John 4:1 tells us to test the spirits to discern what is clear. Discernment comes from alertness, prayer, sensitivity, and listening to a still small voice. If you appeal to God for constant wisdom and discernment, God will give it to you.

More than five hundred years after Nehemiah was opposed, there was someone else who wouldn't come down. King Herod tried to kill Him before He arrived. From the cradle to the cross, He faced endless opposition. He faced misrepresentation. His enemies called Him Satan. But He said, "My kingdom is not of this world" (John 18:36 NKJV). His own disciple Peter tried to keep Him from going to the cross, but He had a discernment that said, "Satan, get thee behind me" (Matthew 16:23 KJV).

Even at the cross, there were those who tried to get

Him to come down. They said, "If You are the Son of God, come down" (Matthew 27:40). The chief priests, scribes, and elders, just like Sanballat, Tobias, and Geshem, were trying to get Him to come down. They were taunting Him, jeering Him, and mocking Him. He had already come down from heaven to the cross. He had already come down from the celestial to the terrestrial. Yet they wanted Him to come down three feet more, which tells us that for some people you can never come down far enough. Don't let people make you do that.

It was important in 444 B.C. that Nehemiah chose not come down. But it was vastly more important that another leader in that same city 470 years later didn't come down. I'm glad that Jesus did not come down. If He had come down, my soul wouldn't have been saved, and your soul wouldn't have been saved, either. Because He didn't come down, we're saved and delivered today. §

Chapter 9
"God Will Not Forget"
(Nehemiah 7)

There are lists of many people who have given sacrificially for important causes. Visitors can view a black-stone memorial in Washington, D.C., honoring a long list of those who sacrificed their lives in World Wars I and II. There is also a monument for those who have given their lives in the Vietnam War. Colleges and universities list names of donors on their walls. The New York Metropolitan Museum has etched in stone the names of their founding donors.

But are these the most significant lists you can get your name on? A hundred years from now, people won't even remember who they are. They'll just look at those names and say, "Who is that?" Even some of the most prominent, wealthiest people of all time will be forgotten. Just think about it. A hundred years from now, will those lists really even matter? No, they'll be forgotten in the sands of time. But how would you like to get on a list that will last forever? We have such a list in Nehemiah 7. It's a list of those who had given their service to God. Thousands of years later we're still reading this list.

In verse 2 Nehemiah assigned his brother Hanani to

govern Jerusalem and designated faithful men to command the fortress. Then Nehemiah took a census of those in exile who had returned to Jerusalem and Judah, naming and numbering them (v. 6).

This shows us that no individual contribution is lost in the mind of God. Whatever you do for God, God knows. As He said to the church of Philadelphia and other churches in Asia Minor in the apostle John's vision, "I know your works" (Revelation 2 and 3 NKJV). God knows our work, both collectively and individually. We tend to think that life is like a vapor that quickly disappears, and in a sense, it is.

Nehemiah 7 contains a long list of unpronounceable names of people who lived twenty-four hundred years ago, but we can still read about them and their contribution. It's reassuring to know that God never loses track of the contribution of any single person in His kingdom. Hebrews 6:10 (NKJV) says, "God . . . will not forget your work and your labor of love."

The work that Nehemiah was doing was organic, like a tree. It took root, grew, and bore fruit. A lasting work for God takes root in a plan. The entire chapter demonstrates that Nehemiah had a plan, a strategy for the work.

After the wall was completed, Nehemiah administrated the work in the city and provinces. He did this with a plan. Dr. Gardner C. Taylor sagaciously once suggested, "It is better to fail with a plan than to succeed without one." The reason is that if you fail with a plan, at least you know where to start in the future.

Creation was a plan that covered seven days. In the first three days, God formed the world, and in the last three days He filled what He formed. But it was still a plan.

Salvation was a plan. God was in Christ reconciling the world to Himself (2 Corinthians 5:19). It was not a haphazard event or secondary scheme, but it was the plan of the Lord to redeem His people. The Lamb was slain before the foundation of the world (Revelation 13:8), and while we were yet sinners Christ died for us (Romans 5:8), because salvation was a plan.

You need a plan for your life, marriage, family, children, business, and career. Proverbs 29:18 says that without a vision, the people perish. For without a plan, the vision perishes. Nehemiah's original plan was to build the wall, but then he formed a plan that will outlast and outlive him and the world.

In his book entitled *Hope Is Not a Strategy*, Rick Page basically suggests that you can't just hope that things will turn out right. You can't just say, "I hope that I will graduate from college, I hope that I will be a successful student, I hope I will have a successful career, I hope I will raise successful children." Hope is not a strategy.

The best-selling book in the history of the United States is *The Purpose Driven Life*, by Rick Warren. I submit that one of the reasons why it's the best-selling book in U.S. history is because it's built around a plan.

A lasting work for God takes root in a plan, but it grows by trusting others to help do the work. Nehemiah delegated some of the work to his brother Hanani and others. Nehemiah trusted an approved person with his work. Every mentor has to walk away, and all mentees have to walk away from their mentors and stand on their own. No one can do all the work. Every great leader will have to put the work into the hands of others.

Hanani was the same brother in chapter 1 who came and explained what was going on with the people because the walls were down. Apparently, Nehemiah saw in his brother a heart of concern, compassion, and commitment. He felt comfortable leaving the work in his hands while he went back to Persia.

There are other biblical role models for this delegation of work. Moses, the titanic figure of the Old Testament, couldn't carry out God's plan for the exodus without Miriam, Aaron, Joshua, and others.

There was a time when Moses tried to do it all (Exodus 18). Moses would spend all day judging small matters brought to him by the people. But when his father-in-law Jethro saw that, he pulled Moses aside and told him that wasn't good. These were really civil cases that he was judging, so Jethro advised him to appoint people who would be in charge of the small matters. Moses could now focus on larger matters.

Jesus did not even try to do it all. Jesus, the Son of God, selected twelve men. Even the Son of God had to trust others to do the work. In Luke 10, Jesus sent out the seventy to do ministry.

In 2 Timothy 1:13-15, Paul essentially told Timothy, "Pattern your preaching after me. Preach the gospel, preach the truth. For there are some who will say that the gospel is not true. Preach the gospel. There are some that will distort it, but pattern your preaching after me." And then he said, "Pass it on to others who will be faithful, who will be qualified to teach other people. Pattern your preaching after me, and then pass it on to others who will protect it—those who are faithful, dependable, and reliable. Pass it on to those who have integrity, fidelity, and sincerity. But don't keep it to yourself. Don't try to do it all yourself. Pass it on so that your ministry will have a legacy."

Let this be a warning to those of you who feel that the work won't get done unless you do it by yourself. Moses, the apostle Paul, and Jesus Christ did not try to do it all by themselves. The reason and rationale for this is that you serve in a kingdom, not an empire. So it is important to ask yourself if you are building a kingdom or an empire. If you're an empire-builder, you'll have to do it all yourself. But if you're a kingdom-builder, you can't do it all yourself. Are you interested in your little program, or God's big mission? If you're interested in your little program, you can do it all yourself. But if you're interested in God's big mission, it's impossible to do it all yourself.

There's a story about the neurotic rooster. He noticed that when the sun came up, he crowed, and the farmer and his wife got up to begin their day. But then he made a fatal deduction. He thought that instead of crowing because the sun came up, the sun came up because he crowed. He became an insomniac. He was afraid that he would oversleep and the sun wouldn't come up; therefore, the farmer wouldn't get up, and his wife and others wouldn't get up either. Finally they carried him to a home for disturbed roosters, where he lived out the rest of his neurotic days—all because he thought the sunrise depended on him alone.

A great work for God takes root in the plan and grows by trusting others with the work, but then it bears the fruit of participation and contribution that's recognized. There were all kinds of people who were recognized, including the priests, the Levites, and the servants. He added all these names up in verse 66. They were less than tribes; instead, they were family groups. It's like walking through a Jewish cemetery or mausoleum for people who lived twenty-four hundred years ago. Yet humans cannot recognize all the individual contributions made in history.

As we look back over our expansive history, we are limited, myopic, nearsighted people. We cannot possibly discern the contribution of every person, other than a handful of great, noted leaders. But God doesn't have that impediment or frustration. He knows the contribution of every person. When we listen to a symphony, we really can't distinguish every individual contribution of every musician, but God knows. Football teams comprise trainers, coaches, linemen, water boys, fifty-two members on the team, along with an office staff and publicity staff, but only a few will hold the trophy. Only a few will get the sponsorships and jersey sales, even though the Super Bowl is the most watched athletic game of the year. Even though only a few from the winning team will get a chance to hold the trophy and receive the sponsorships, the entire team comprises a lot more people than the eleven men on the football field.

Some people get overlooked for the work they do, but there are some who get credit for work that they don't do. But God will not forget your work and labor of love. In 2 Corinthians 5:10, Paul says that we all must appear before the *bema*, the judgment seat of Christ. It is not a judgment seat for salvation but rather an evaluation of contributions of work. Each one will see the things that have been done in his body. Some people spend their whole Christian lives dipping and dodging, hiding behind the labor of others, acting like they're doing something.

But one day there's going to be an account of what we actually have done. Some people who have been overlooked are going to get a reward, and some who have taken credit for stuff they didn't do will be exposed. Each one must appear before the judgment seat, so we can't hide behind someone else. The work for God takes root in a plan, grows by sharing responsibility, and bears the fruit of recognition by someone else.

In his book, *Man's Search for Meaning*, Viktor Frankl tells of his experience as a Jew who survived the concentration camp. He says that those who survived were the ones who had a sense of significance and meaning. They had a purpose for living. Those who died had no sense of significance. They didn't feel that their life mattered.

Where do you find significance? Where do you find the will to keep going on? Everyone longs to be a part of something meaningful. Whether you're a CEO who thinks significance means owning mansions all over world, or a teenager who finds significance wearing the colors and tattoo of a gang, each one of you wants to feel important.

There's nothing wrong with prestige or power, if that's what you desire. The problem with it is that there will always be somebody more significant than you. There will always be someone with more money, a bigger house, and more expensive cars. Someone will always be more intelligent or better looking than you.

But there's another way to find significance, and that's in work for the kingdom of God. Why not be a part of something that will last forever? §

Chapter 10

Recovery of the Word

(Nehemiah 8)

There is an excitement in the recovery of things. A worldwide sensation erupted when the biblical manuscripts known as the Dead Sea Scrolls were found in 1948. There was a tremendous excitement when archaeologist Howard Carter found the tomb of King Tutankhamun. But no discovery was as thrilling as the recovery of the Pentateuch (the books of Moses, the first five books of the Bible) when it was found in 444 B.C., nearly twenty-four hundred years ago.

The people had come back from Babylon and rebuilt the wall in fifty-two days. They were now ready for the purpose of building the wall—to introduce the Word of God again. Ezra the priest stood on a wooden platform in front of the Water Gate and read the books of the Law to the people. As Ezra read, the Levites explained the meaning of the passages being read. The people wept as they heard the Law read, but Ezra, Nehemiah, and the Levites told them to rejoice since it was a sacred day. They instructed the people to celebrate and feast together.

It's the same for us. The recovery of the Bible gives

us the lens to see the living God. It helps us to encounter God in a fresh and meaningful way. Like the people in 444 B.C., we need to recover the Word of God in our own lives because powerful things will happen. The question is this: would the discovery of God's Word in our life create excitement for us? How many times has the recovery of just a single book been powerful?

One day St. Augustine heard the children singing, "Take the Word and read it." He looked down at the Bible that was opened to the Book of Romans. He read it, and this led to his conversion. Luther had been meditating on the Book of Romans when he affirmed the doctrine of justification by faith. John Wesley had been sitting at the gate, reading the preface to the book by Luther on Romans, and his heart was strangely warmed. It was the biggest theological bombshell in a hundred years. Karl Barth rediscovered the Book of Romans and wrote his own commentary in 1919. All of these historical examples prove that just the recovery of one book of the Bible is powerful and significant.

There was a recovery of the Word of God communally in verse 1 of our text. This was not a private reading; instead, this was a community hearing for all the people coming together as one. In the whole history of Christianity, there has been a distinct difference between the public and private reading of the Word of God. It's almost forgotten today in Christian worship. From the post-apostolic time to the era of the apostolic fathers, to the Patristic Period on through the Roman Catholic Period, Orthodoxy, and so forth, the public reading of the Word of God in the community of God has been a central act of worship. Indeed, it's good to read the Bible in your own prayer closets—in your own altar time, meditation time, or devotional time. But there is a qualitative difference in the public reading and hearing of the Word of God, and that's why we read it publicly.

Dr. Charles Campbell, a mainline Presbyterian who teaches at Duke Divinity School, has taken to the public reading of the Word of God. He and some students once stood outside an emergency room at Grace Hospital in Atlanta and just read the Word of God. He had students read the Beatitudes out loud at the Atlanta MTA at midnight. They not only read it communally, but they also read the Word of God publicly.

There is a witness to others in just reading the Bible in public. This doesn't necessarily mean you have to read the Word of God out loud, but just open it up and read it in public. This has an enormous impact, whether you're riding on an airplane, waiting at a train or bus station, or eating at a coffee shop. One of my fellow pastors was running late one day, and he had some stops to make in town. He ran into the bank to deposit a check, forgetting that he had his Bible with him. He wasn't even thinking about it. When he went up to the teller, he just put the Bible on the counter. He said that the teller's eyes got so big, you would have thought he put a bomb there. Just by laying on that bank counter, the actual Bible had great power and influence. This story shows that just the very presence of the Bible has impact.

For Nehemiah's people, *the recovery of the Word was continuous*. They read the Bible from morning to midday. It's not like Brylcreem, the hair product that advertised, "A little dab will do you." No, they stood for hours, focused on the continuous hearing of the Word of God, until it became intolerably hot. It was not like the members of our congregations of today who get impatient for a seat if they stand too long in the lobby. The Hebrews of Nehemiah's day stood, allowing sufficient time for hearing the Word of God.

There is a continual need for the Word of God. Jesus said, "Man shall not live by bread alone but by every word that proceedeth out of the mouth of God" (Matthew 4:4 KJV). Romans 10:17 (NKJV) tells us, "Faith comes by hearing [continuously], and hearing by the Word of God." The psalmist said, "Blessed is the man that walketh not in the counsel of the ungodly, nor standeth in the way of sinners, nor sitteth in the seat of the scornful. But his delight is in the law of the Lord;

and in his law doth he meditate day and night" (Psalm 1:1-2 KJV). In other words, you should think about the Word continuously, in the day when it is clear and you can see your way, but also in the night when you are unsure. Meditate on it!

This verse suggests the idea of a cow that chews its cud. A cow, which has several stomachs, chews the cud, digests it in one stomach, and then regurgitates. It then chews more nutrients and digests it to a second stomach, even a third, and continues this process to get all the nutrients out of it. Job 23:12 essentially says, "I want Your word more than my necessary food." In other words, reading God's Word and then meditating on it needs to be continuous.

Also, for the Hebrews on that day *the recovery of the Word was conspicuous*. In verse 5, Ezra went up to the platform and opened the Word so the people might see it. He was standing above the people, and they looked up at him. He was in the middle of the square, in the middle of the city, and the people stood up. IT was conspicuous. In post-modern days, we've almost hidden the Bible in the church house, as if it was chained to the cathedral pulpit like in the high Catholic churches of the Middle Ages.

Dr. Carl Bates, our former president of the Southern Baptist Convention and pastor of the First Baptist

Church in Amarillo, testified that before he was saved, he went to a hotel with a plan to commit suicide. He opened up the drawer, and there was a Gideon Bible. He took it out and started to read it. He read about how much God loved him and sent His Son to die for him. That night he accepted Christ into his life, just by reading the Word of God that was conspicuously present. The conspicuous Word of God is indeed powerful.

They recovered the Word, and it was read reverently. In verse 6, they stood up and said, "Amen, Amen!" Amen means, "So be it." It was a word of affirmation. They lifted their heads and then bowed in worship with their faces to the ground. They wept so much when they heard the Word that Ezra, Nehemiah, and the Levites had to tell them to stop crying. They did this out of holy reverence and respect for the Word of God.

There ought to be a reverence for God's Word, even during the worship service. When the gospel is preached and the Word is read, there should be no walking around in the sanctuary or lobby. When the Word is read, even in Sunday school, the people should show reverence, a genuine respect for God's Word.

A fellow pastor told a story about being on vacation. He rented a car and drove to his hotel. The next morning the valet brought his car back around because he was going to spend the day out. The car looked exactly like the same make, model, and color as the one he rented, but when he got into the front seat he just felt something was different and strange. But then he remembered that when he picked the car up, he had a small Bible with him that he put in the glove compartment. He opened up the compartment, but the Bible was not in it. He said that since the Word was not in it, he got out of it. Likewise, anything the Word is not in, you need to get out of, whether it's a relationship, job, or career. Whatever it is, if the Word is not in it, you need to get out of it.

The people recovered the Word intelligently. They had been in Babylon for seventy years, so there was a mixture of languages that they brought back—a patois, if you will, of Hebrew and Babylonian languages that became Aramaic. When the Levites read the pure biblical Hebrew, they had to help the people understand it on their own. Because they had lost the use of the Hebrew language while they were in exile, the priests did what it took for them to hear the Word intelligently. You need to intelligently understand what the Word means, and then you can make a clear, direct application of it.

In the Book of Acts, Philip approached the Ethiopian who was reading Isaiah and asked him, "Do you understand it?" The Ethiopian replied, "How can I understand it unless somebody teaches me?" (Acts 8:30-31). The Word of God must be read intelligently.

There's an old television show called "Gunsmoke" that ran from 1955 to 1975 and still airs on TV Land reruns. It featured Marshal Matt Dillon in Dodge City. In this particular episode, Matt Dillon had an illiterate assistant deputy named Festus Haggen. Festus was an American icon, but he was illiterate—he couldn't read. He was called out as a sworn deputy official when this couple wanted to get married. He said he could not marry them unless there was a Bible. So they searched everywhere, up and down, for the Book and finally found one. He married them and pronounced them man and wife. But the stunning thing was that in the last scene of the episode, when the camera zoomed in on the book, it was not the Bible but Louisa May Alcott's novel, *Little Women*. He used the book, but he did not understand what he was using. In the same way, we've got to read the Book intelligently.

The people recovered the Word in a celebratory way. In verse 10, the Levites cheered them, saying, "The joy of the Lord is your strength." They responded by holding a feast and celebrating in verse 12. They ate and drank because they understood the words they were declaring. They rejoiced greatly. Likewise, after you have heard the Word and understood it, it's time to celebrate because you know that the joy of the Lord is your strength.

Notice this about the joy of the Lord: Joy is different

from happiness. Happiness is based on what's happening around you. But joy, as one of the fruit of the Spirit, comes from the inside. Regardless of outside circumstances, you can still have joy. Even if you're sick, He's a doctor; if you're in trouble, He's a lawyer. That's joy. Isaiah 40:31 says, "They that wait on the Lord shall renew their strength." And your strength, in turn, shall give you joy.

In Ethiopia there's a tribe call the Walamos. Missionaries arrived there right before World War II. When Mussolini invaded the area, he deposed the emperor, Haile Selassie. The missionaries were basically run out of the area. But they left this little tribe a copy of the Bible, and after the war, when Haile Selassie was reinstated as king by his allies, the missionaries returned. To their absolute astonishment, by just leaving that one Bible, thousands of Walamos had been converted and started churches. When they left, forty-eight people had been converted, but when they returned, over eighteen thousand had been converted. They left them with the Bible, and when they came back after World War II, a whole community had been transformed.

In fact, the natives had no one to interpret the Bible for them. When they read Philippians 3:2, which says, "Beware of the dogs," the Walamos took it literally and killed all the dogs in the region. That's how serious they were about following the Word of God. But this story testifies to the power of the unaided work of God.

The Walamos had endured the worst and weakest circumstances. They were ravaged by war, persecuted and sold by the Italian army, and abandoned by the missionaries who had not even gotten started converting them. But just leaving the Bible with them converted a whole culture.

Just leave the Word of God on your table, desk, or car. Wherever it is, the Word of God is able to convert and transform your life. §

Chapter 11

One for All, All for One

(Nehemiah 9:38—10:1-27, 30)

He died in a dirty, little concentration camp on April 9, 1945. He was one of the most brilliant young pastors and theologians of the twentieth century. His writings challenge us to address the presence of God in the world among history. His courageous resistance against Hitler, along with his imprisonment and execution, dramatized his commitment to Christ. He could have escaped; he didn't have to face punishment. But as an individual he went back and stayed with God's people. What made him do it? What made him go back? Perhaps our text will give us some insight.

"All Scripture is inspired [breathed out by God] and it is profitable for teaching, reproof, correction, training in righteousness," according to 1 Timothy 3:16 (NRSV). This means that all of the Scriptures have a practical application for our lives today. All of them, whether it's a list of names as dry as dust or a beautiful display of poetry from one of the Psalms or the prophets, have great value for us. Perhaps you have felt this way when studying the Book of Nehemiah.

In chapter 10 we discover a special document that

was written and signed by Nehemiah, the Levites, political leaders, gatekeepers, singers, temple servants, and others. This document recorded promises that had been made after the people confessed their sins to God. They prayed a prayer of confession, and now they made this commitment.

This document is a wonderful example of the need that many people feel to put into written form the new direction they want to take in life. The new covenant, or agreement, that Israel made with God to follow the Word and His precepts was followed by a list of signers. First of all, Nehemiah the governor signed it. Accompanying his signature were the names of priests, a group called Levites. Those who served in the temple also signed the agreement. The names of a group of leaders were listed, followed by the rulers, the nobles of the land, and finally the common people. Verses 1 through 27 of chapter 10 underscore the importance of taking individual responsibility for one's actions, which matters greatly to God.

Twenty-four hundred years later, these individuals' names are not lost in time but preserved in the Holy Scriptures. As a company of the committed, these people saw the need for preserving and perpetuating changes in their lifestyle in order to keep in step with God. Thus, they signed this agreement to bind themselves to the end.

The agreement represents the universal urge among humans to publicly pledge to be loyal to the cause they feel is right. In many instances this kind of record in biblical history is the case. This list and all lists like it in the Word of God for all time and eternity remind us that God is not just a God of the collective, but He is also the God of the individual.

Rudyard Kipling, in his poem "Tomlinson," says, "Though we called your friend from his bed last night, he could not speak for you. For the race is run by one and one and never by two and two."

Dr. Gardner C. Taylor said, "We enter this world as an individual, and we leave this world as an individual, one at a time. While we are here, we are part of a community. The gospel that ends with the individual ends. But when you look at individual personhood and life at the beginning, we come into the world one at a time, and we leave one at a time."

We are part of a collective group, yet our decision for Christ is an individual commitment and decision. There is no group plan to glory. Oftentimes, if you have a group of employees, there's a group plan for insurance. That's great for insurance, but it does not work for blessed assurance. No, you have to make an individual commitment and decision for Christ. You may ask some people if they're saved and know Jesus. They respond, "My mother and grandmother were saved, my father was a preacher and my grandfather was a deacon." But you cannot hitchhike your way to heaven on your family's testimony. You have to know God for yourself.

It's as if in these last verses God has made a motion, and every one of us have to second that motion with his or her signature. We don't do it with our physical signatures, but we do it with our lives. There's no way to escape the private and personal commitment to Christ. It matters to God that we live distinctive lives.

The signers of the covenant also committed themselves to avoid being unequally yoked in marriage. In verse 30 they promised not to give their daughters in marriage to people around them, nor take their daughters for their own sons. We must not interpret this verse with morbid literalism. Instead, we must understand that there were individuals from nations around them that did not follow God. Because they were caught up in idolatry, connecting with those foreign nations would've turned the children of Israel back to those same practices that got them in trouble in the first place.

Moabite and Amalekites lived around the area. For our purposes today, the issue is not so much concerning the Amalekites and Moabites without, as much as it is the Amalekites and Moabites within. So, we need to guard ourselves from internal issues and problems that would cause us not to live distinctive lives for God. The apostle Paul said it like this: "I find then a law, that, when I would do good, evil is present with me. For I delight in the law of God after the inward man: but I see another law in my members, warring against the law of my mind, and bringing me into captivity to the law of sin which is in my members" (Romans 7:23).

So the people agreed first of all to live distinctive lives. In the same way, as Christians we should avoid anything that might dampen our witness or cause us not to be distinctive. Jesus said in the Sermon on the Mount that we are the salt of the earth and the light of the world. If salt loses its saltiness, then it will no longer be salty. Neither does one put a light under the bushel (Matthew 5:13-15). Salt that has lost its flavor represents the loss of distinctiveness through accommodation. So anything that causes our salt to lose its saltiness or our light to be dimmed should be avoided.

Ralph Salmon said that there is an old hypocrisy and a new hypocrisy. The old hypocrisy back in the Victorian era was acting better than you really were, but in this era it seems the new hypocrisy involves acting worse than we really are. We must remember that 1 Peter 2:9 (KJV) says that we are "a chosen generation, a royal priesthood, an holy nation, a peculiar people; that we should shew forth the praises of him who hath called you out of darkness into his marvellous light."

It matters to God that we live in community. There's a significance in the temple of the Jewish community because it has always represented a collective experience of God together. The temple was an absolute, visible reality to the Jews about everything regarding their faith. The psalmist cried in Psalm 27:4 that he wanted to go back and dwell in the house of the Lord, in the temple. Even Jonah speaks about the fact that there is a temple. From the belly of the whale, he said, "While I was fainting away, I remembered the Lord; and my prayer came to Thee, into Thy holy temple" (Jonah 2:7). There was a manifest presence of God in the temple.

All of us must recognize that we are supposed to be a part of the community, a part of the temple. The first sin in Genesis was the breaking of community. God came walking in the cool of the day and said, "Adam, where are you?" In other words, He was asking, "Why have you broken communion?" The second sin was addressed when God asked Cain, "Where is your brother?" and Cain replied, "Am I my brother's keeper?" Again, it was the breaking of community that was the primordial sin.

Hebrews 10:25 says "not [to forsake] the assembling of yourselves together." Some say that you don't have to go to church to be a Christian, which is true, but because you're a Christian, you ought to go to church. LeBron James doesn't need to go to the gym to be a basketball player, but if he's going to score every now and then, he needs to go to the gym. A doctor doesn't have to go to the hospital to be a doctor, but if they're going to operate, they ought to be going to the hospital. A chef doesn't have to go to the kitchen to be a chef, but if he's going to cook anything, then he needs to go to the kitchen. There's beauty and wonder, along with purpose and power, in community.

And finally, there is the support of the temple in community. From time immemorial, the worship of God has always been in community. The purpose of worship is not just to come together but also to bring an offering, in particular, the tithe. Even the pagans, including the Babylonians, Persians, and Greeks, paid tithes to their gods. The tithe has always been inextricably tied to the community.

If you love the community, then you'll understand God's purpose in the collective experience of tithing. Everywhere they understood that being a part of the community meant to support it financially. David once said, "I will not offer to God that which cost me nothing" (2 Samuel 24:24). It matters to God that there's an individual responsibility, it matters to God that we live a life of distinction, but it also matters to God that we live in community with one another.

Adolf Hitler seduced a nation and attempted to exterminate the Jews from Europe. A small number of dissidents worked to dismantle the Third Reich from the inside. This particular pastor and author worked against Hitler's regime. For doing that, he and a third of the ministers were stripped of their credentials.They couldn't marry, they couldn't bury, they couldn't baptize, and they couldn't serve Communion. That pastor's name was Dietrich Bonhoeffer.

Bonhoeffer stayed true to his commitment to community. He ran an underground seminary associated with the Free Anglican faith and wrote a book there called *Life Together*. The Christian experience, he said, is about life together. This same sense of community sustained him and virtually helped him to work against Hitler and ultimately defeat him. It sustained him when he had a chance to escape to New York but decided to go back and stand with the German church. This sense of community sustained him when he was in the prison Tegel in Berlin. It also sustained him as he moved from one concentration camp to another.

On the other hand, he was also a great individual in history. He made an individual commitment to God, but he also made a commitment to community. Committed to the faith regardless, he was so committed to community that on his way to the scaffold in Flossenbürg, he was heard encouraging other prisoners and praying for them. He led a powerful service the night before with the inmates, and observers heard him praying for the prisoners.

The interesting thing about Bonhoeffer is that the Germans didn't really recognize him as Bonhoeffer. They hung him in an ugly, little concentration camp in Flossenbürg, where he died. In other words, he was just another prisoner and protester. Fifty years later, a Nazi doctor who saw Bonhoeffer at the gallows described his death. He said Pastor Bonhoeffer knelt on the floor and prayed fervently to God, and it was the most moving thing he had ever seen. He'd never seen anyone die like Bonhoeffer, entirely submissive to the will of God. There's a line in *Life Together* in which Bonhoeffer expresses the fact we need one another. He said, "The Christ in you is stronger than the Christ in me. When I'm weak, I need the Christ in you, and when you're weak, you need the Christ in me." §

Chapter 12

Praising God at the Garbage Dump

(Nehemiah 12)

Dmitri Shostakovich, a great Russian composer in the twentieth century during World War II, was also a patriot. He wanted to serve his country, but they didn't want the most famous composer in the country on the front lines. So they created a job position for him to make him feel good. He had the responsibility of guarding the roof of the music conservatory in St. Petersburg, which is called Leningrad today. When the Germans were bombing Leningrad, which was under their siege for days, Shostakovich was working at the time on composing a magnificent symphony while wearing a helmet on top of the roof. As the bombs came down, sometimes part of the roof would catch on fire. He would have to go over, put out the fire, and come back to finish writing his music. He wrote music as a celebration in the midst of a confrontation. Right there on the roof, he was putting out fires and writing music while celebrating in the midst of opposition.

The latter part of chapter 12 describes a dedication of the wall of Jerusalem, a wonderful event that evidently had been postponed for a while until the city could be filled with people again. Now the project was complete.

The wall was built, and the gates were hung. It was now a well-defended and beautiful city filled with people. The time had come for the dedication and celebration of the wall.

In this passage we have an account of a great processional around the top of the wall. There were choir musicians, officials, and politicians on hand at the event. In the aftermath of the work of God, the people of God paused and celebrated. They didn't have to do this. In fact, they could have just gone right in and kept busy, opening up restaurants and farms. But they thought it was important to pause and mark an important moment in their history.

All meaningful activity begins with a significant pause. Socrates insightfully and sagaciously suggested that the "unexamined life is not worth living." We live in an instant, rapid society, but occasionally we should pause. Everything is going at such an accelerated pace that whenever something great happens to us, there's a temptation to rush. Yet there's power in a significant pause. It's important for us to reflect, pause, and examine.

For example, you don't begin major events without some kind of pause. In baseball the pitcher goes to the mound, but he doesn't just start pitching the ball. No, he pauses and looks away to see if perhaps someone is trying to steal a base, or sometimes he'll take a moment to focus his vision. But his pitching begins with a pause. Even in a football game, the punter prepares for the kick off. He doesn't just run and kick the ball. No, he holds up his hand to get everyone's attention first. Then he and his team run toward the ball and the opposing team. What makes a symphony great is not the barrage of notes; instead, it's the rests that are strategically placed throughout the musical piece to produce pauses. Without these rests, great music would not be as great or enjoyable. In a doctor's office you don't move from the front door to the examination room. No, you pause first in what's called a waiting room.

There's a waiting ritual even in Buckingham Palace and the palace at Wales. You never run into the presence of the king. Rather, you go from a smaller room to a larger room and then into another larger room. Finally you're in the throne room. You walk into a succession of larger rooms to prepare you for who you're about to see.

And that's what's going on here in the celebration of the building of the wall in Jerusalem. First of all, they paused to mark this moment that signified what God had done and prepared them for what was going to happen in the future.

Second, it was a time not only of pause, but also a time of praise. The choirs, instrumentalists, and singers gathered together to give God praise. Chapter 12 describes cymbals, stringed instruments, harps, and singing, all giving God glorious praise. This was important, not just something to be done out of ceremony. No, this was a significant, integral part of the dedication. It's not like "The Star-Spangled Banner" sung at the beginning of a ball game, which is a perfunctory patriotic act. The National Anthem, written in 1812 about the battle of Fort McHenry, has absolutely nothing to do with what's about to happen.

Not so with this time of joyful celebration. This passage of Scripture lets us know that praise is not extraneous or superfluous. No, it's a powerful and important part of our worship. David said, "Enter into His gates with thanksgiving, and into His courts with praise, be thankful unto him and bless His name. For the Lord is good; His mercy is everlasting; and His truth endureth to all generations" (Psalm 100:4-5 KJV).

These people were happy because they were finished; their objective had been reached. God had given them the power to gain the victory to accomplish something. Similarly, when God blesses us, we ought to pause and give thanks to Him. We ought to thank Him for what He allowed us to accomplish. We ought to be able to stand on top of whatever God has allowed us to accomplish and give Him praise.

The Hebrews had marked a point of pause and a period of praise. Finally, they were honoring God at a peculiar place. They were worshiping God not at a temple, not at the cathedral, but at the Dung Gate (v. 31). There were other gates where they could have praised Him, like the Water Gate or the Sheep Gate, but they decided to do it at the Dung Gate. At that place stinking of muck and debris, they stood on top of the refuse gate and had a thanksgiving concert. In the same way, you ought to be able to stand on top of the stinky stuff and give God praise.

Is that not what happened in John 11? Jesus had spent two extra days at His present location after hearing that His friend Lazarus was sick. Lazarus died, and He showed up after Lazarus was buried. Martha said, "If You had been here, my brother would not have died." And Jesus said to her, "You will see your brother again." Martha said, "I know I will see him in the resurrection." Jesus said, "I am the resurrection." Then He said, "Show Me where you laid him." (In other words, "Show Me where you gave up.) As Martha was preparing to show Him, she said, "He stinketh." Essentially Jesus said, "I won't let the stink stop Me."

Stinky situations don't stop Jesus. And we have some stinky things in our past. But I'm glad I serve a Savior that won't let the stink stop Him. Even in the midst of stinky stuff, Nehemiah's people were able to give God praise. There are some foul, stinky situations in your life, but you ought to be able to look past them and give God glory and praise.

There were two teenagers in Indianapolis, Indiana, who were sleeping in one of those large garbage containers outside. It just so happened that the next morning was the trash pick-up day. When the teens heard the truck preparing to grab the bin to put them into the garbage truck, that's when they woke up, but they didn't wake up in time to get out of the garbage bin. So they were stuck in the garbage truck before they started screaming and hollering. The man in the garbage truck heard them, stopped the truck, and rescued them.

In the same way, you've got to keep praising God, because everything in the trash is not bad; there is some valuable stuff in the garbage. So even if you find yourself in a garbage situation, a stinky situation, or a foul circumstance, give God praise because He is able to rescue you out of the trash. §

NOTES